BRITISH COLUMBIA

JOSEF HANUS & JOSEF M. HANUS

Personal gift to:

Jim

From: Jim – A Small
Momento of Your
Journey to Lala Land!
Ron 12 July 2008

Vancouver Island

British Columbia's largest island, located in the extreme southwest part of the province, is some 460 kilometres long and up to 90 kilometres wide. At 32,200 square kilometers, the island, which is separated from the mainland near the Strait of Georgia, is the largest island off the west coast of both North and South America. Connection to and from the island is provided by BC Ferries from Horseshoe Bay in West Vancouver as well as from Tsawwassen. The ferry trip takes 100 minutes and is a memorable experience for travelers. This picture, taken from a ferry, shows Piers Island and Colburne Passage. Victoria's BC Ferries terminal is located in Swartz Bay in North Saanich, providing trips to Tsawwassen approximately every two hours, and several daily connections to the Gulf Islands. Some ferry lines also provide connections from Crofton, Nanaimo and Chemanius to numerous other locations on the mainland.

2

Saanich Inlet

Satellite Channel, Saanich Inlet with Central Saanich and Brentwood Bay with Mount Baker grace the background of this picture, taken from the scenic lookout on the Trans-Canada Highway. Saanich Inlet is located in the southernmost part of Vancouver Island, north of Victoria.

Thunderbird Park

Native totem poles can be found all over Victoria. One of the highest, carved by a team led by Kwakiutl tribal chief Mungo Martin, was erected in Beacon Hill Park in 1956 and stood there until 2000. Another totem pole known as the Spirit of Lekwammen was raised in 1994 and stood until 1997. The Spirit of Lekwammen was almost 55 metres high. This picture shows totem poles in Thunderbird Park, near the Legislature Buildings.

3

BC Region: CAPITAL
Vancouver Island

Victoria

This global tourist destination and British Columbia's capital city, located on the southernmost tip of Vancouver Island, began its rich history in the late 1700s, when Coast Salish people settled here. First settled as Fort Camosun in 1843 by Hudson's Bay Company, the settlement came to be called Fort Victoria.

BC Parliament Buildings

The seat of British Columbia's government is located in Victoria's Inner Harbour. The buildings, designed in the style of the Romanesque Revival, are considered among the most beautiful in the world. Designed by 25 year old architect Francis Rattenbury after the Englishman won the government's design competition, the buildings were completed in 1898.

4

Cadboro Point

Strolling the rocky beaches of Victoria's shores, you will find breathtaking ocean views between Ross Bay and Cordova Bay.

Craigdarroch Castle

This Victorian-era mansion was built as the home of coal baron Robert Dunsmuir in the 1890s. The 39-room castle was sold in 1908 and for the next 60 years housed various public institutions. The building, situated near the downtown harbour, has been restored in recent years and is now owned by the Craigdarroch Castle Historical Museum Society and is open to the public. Other interesting museums in Victoria are the Royal British Columbia Museum, Maritime Museum of British Columbia, Sooke Region Museum, British Columbia's oldest building, Helmcken House, and the British Columbia Aviation Museum with more than 30 aircraft on display.

5

Gulf Islands

The Saltspring, Denman, Mayne, Saturna, Pender, Gabriola and Galiano are seven well-known islands within the Southern Gulf Island group. Numerous smaller and partially privately owned islands are nestled snug in the southern part of the Georgia Strait between British Columbia's mainland and North Saanich. Spectacular scenery and great outdoor recreation beckon artists, anglers and hikers alike.

Nanaimo Bastion

The most endearing symbol of the "Harbour City" is The Bastion, the oldest original free-standing Hudson's Bay Company fort in North America. It is the oldest building in Nanaimo and the second oldest in British Columbia, the first being Helmcken House, built in 1852 by Sebastian Helmcken in Victoria's centre.

6

Victoria Downtown

Victoria's downtown is the place where old and new architecture stands side by side. The Parliament Buildings, Convention Centre and Royal British Columbia Museum are located in close proximity to contemporary-style apartment buildings.

Empress Hotel

The Empress Hotel is nestled near the Parliament Buildings in Victoria's Inner Harbour. The 460-room hotel was completed in Edwardian-style architecture in 1905 by the Canadian Pacific Railway. The hotel, the most photographed attraction on Vancouver Island, originally opened in 1908 and was recently restored to its original grandeur with luxurious decor and antique furniture. The hotel's grandeur reminds one of the elegance of a bygone era while services and accommodation meet the needs of the contemporary traveler.

7

Nanaimo

The city's history began as a trading post in the early 1800s, and now Nanaimo is the second largest city on Vancouver Island. Nanaimo is home to some 80,000 residents as well as the campus of Malaspina University College, located on scenic slopes above. The city of Nanaimo is located in the mid-southeast part of Vancouver Island, just 100 kilometres north of Victoria. Nanaimo is a major BC Ferries port, connecting the island with Vancouver via Horseshoe Bay. Coal, found on Vancouver's beaches by natives was one of the first items traded with the Hudson's Bay Company. The first trade fort to do business with the European market was established in Nanaimo near Hudson's and the Bastion served as a company office.

Departure Bay

Departure Bay in Nanaimo and BC Ferries port.

8

Cathedral Grove

MacMillan Park, the home of Canada's biggest trees, is a fascinating place for tourists driving to Port Alberni, Long Beach and Tofino. Some of the enormous Coast Douglas Firs are 70 metres high, 1.7 metres in diameter and over 800 years old. Western Red Cedar, Western Hemlock and Sitka Spruce grow here as well in the ancient rainforests of the Pacific Coast. Called Cathedral Grove, the forest is located near Cameron Lake, 25 kilometres from Qualicum Beach.

Port Alberni

The mining and logging town of Port Alberni is nestled in the Alberni Valley at the head of the island's longest inlet. Known as the 'Salmon Capital of the World', its waters boast all five species of Pacific salmon. The most popular fish, at times weighing in at 45 pounds, is the Chinook salmon, also known as the king salmon, tyee salmon, Spring Salmon and blackmouth.

9

Barkley Sound

The Broken Group Islands located south of Ucluelet in Barkley Sound, are a particularly favorite recreation place for paddlers and boaters in the Pacific Rim, providing a true west coast experience in secure water, without extreme ocean conditions. The parks area, covering 800 square kilometres, was first explored in 1787 by Captain Charles Barkley. It is said that Barkley's 17-year old bride Frances was the first white woman ever to lay eyes on British Columbia.

Ucluelet

Ucluelet, situated on the southern end of Long Beach, was originally a First Nation village, occupied by fur sellers and fishermen living at Spring Cove. In 1959 the village was connected with Port Alberni. This picture is of Ucluelet Boat Basin.

10

BC Region: ALBERNI-CLAYOQUOT
Vancouver Island

Long Beach

One million visitors yearly stroll the friendly sandy beaches on the extreme west side of Vancouver Island. Long Beach is 11 kilometres long, and its warm sand can experience rapidly changing weather, from blazing sun to fog and wind in a very short time. Long Beach, the most beautiful part of the Pacific Rim National Park, can easily be reached from Nanaimo via Port Alberni. Long Beach is a great subject for photographers, inspiring the use of challenging techniques such as a fish eye lens, which is what was used for this picture. The trek across the island is also challenging experience.

Amphitrite Point

The lighthouse, built near the southern end of Ucluelet in 1906, is an easily accessible point, with a good view to explore Barkley Sound.

11

Port Hardy

The northernmost town on Vancouver Island is Port Hardy, the gateway to Cape Scott Provincial Park. A BC Ferries port connects Vancouver Island with Prince Rupert and Queen Charlotte Islands and is located in Hardy Bay. The trip through the Inside and Discovery Coast Passages can be started from Vancouver or from Port Hardy. Many visitors choose to whale watching, and can often spot Killer, Grey, Minke and Humpback Whales. The town with some 5,000 residents was named after Vice Admiral Sir Thomas Hardy.

Campbell River

Famous for salmon fishing in crystal clear waters, Discovery Passage is a magnet for fishermen from around the world. A popular annual event is the Salmon Festival held every July.

12

Clayoquot Sound

An impressive tourist spot named Clayoquot Sound just north of Tofino can be reached only by boat or aircraft. This magnificent, mostly wild area of some 350,000 hectares of ocean and land, is made up of five communities with a total population of 3,000, including four First Nation reserves inhabited by the Nuu-chah-nulth First Nation tribe.

Tofino

Visited by millions, the northernmost point of the Pacific Rim Park, Tofino, is located in Clayoquot Sound. A nature lovers' paradise, Tofino brings in thousands of surfers, whale watchers, fishermen and boaters every summer. Next to numerous new restaurants, motels and recreation companies, Tofino offers a first hand experience of the British Columbian pristine wilderness.

13

©Josef Hanus

Nelson Island

The natural beauty of Nelson Island has so far been untouched by modern civilization and the population remains very small. The Island is located west of the Sechelet Peninsula, and is approximately 15 kilometres long. It is only accessible by boat or float-plane. There are no modern services, all shopping, postal services and banking should be done from Powel River on Sunshine Coast. An interesting fact is that Nelson granite was used to build the Parliament Buildings in Victoria as well as some buildings in Vancouver and the Victoria Harbour sea wall.

Texada Island

Located along the Sunshine Coast, Texada Island, measuring in at 50 kilometeres, is the largest of the Gulf Islands. Spectacular views of the Coast Mountains and Vancouver Island can be seen from this island.

14

Skookumchuck Narrows

The Narrows are located at the mouth of the Sechelet Inlet near Jarvis Inlet and is a memorable spot for hikers and a challenge for white-water kayakers. The waters of the Pacific Ocean are constricted at the narrows as they ebb and flow each day; the extreme difference between high and low tide resulting in an amazing spectacle of rapids.

Gibsons

The gateway to Sunshine Coast is Gibsons, where a BC Ferries port is located. The trip from the Lower Mainland involves 40 minutes of beautiful views of the shores dotted by hundreds of homes and cottages. In the past, forestry and fishing were the main interest of Sunshine Coast residents, however nowadays tourism plays an important economic part. Gibsons, pictured here, has 4,000 residents.

15

Sunshine Coast

The Lions

The Coast Mountains form a dramatic backdrop to the city below, stretching from Howe Sound to Indian Arm and reaching heights of 1,500 metres. The twin peaks, 'The Lions,' named for their resemblance to the Landseer Lions in London's Trafalgar Square, stand as silent sentinels over the city.

Brockton Point

Totem poles in Stanley Park in Vancouver include a house post, a memorial pole and a mortuary pole. Some of the most common animals carved on totems poles are the bear, wolf, raven, eagle, frog, killer whale and hawk. Mythical beings also have their place on the totem poles, however totem poles are not religious icons, but rather celebrations of culture. The various people represented with these poles include the Kwakiutl, Haida, Nisgaa and Nuu-chah-nulth.

16

Cypress Mountains

Vancouver has several of Canada's best skiing areas. The most popular skiing area near the city is Cypress Bowl, just 30 minutes from downtown. Excellent terrain for both downhill and cross-country skiing are open to the public day or night from early December to the late spring.

Hollyburn

In addition to skiing, Cypress and Grouse Mountains offer some of the best views of Greater Vancouver. Grouse Mountain is the highest point above Vancouver and can easily be reached from downtown via public transit and Skyride gondola. A third area, Mount Seymour Provincial Park, reaches up into the eastern edge of North Vancouver's rugged mountains. Fine skiing for beginners and the experienced alike can be expected from this area.

17

English Bay

West End is Vancouver's most urban neighbourhood. Within the jungle of apartment buildings that give the city its distinctive skyline, West End is Canada's most densely populated area per square kilometre, stretching west from Burrard Street. Sunny sandy beaches create a beautiful environment along West End and Stanley Park. Pedestrians can enjoy peaceful strolls along the sea or tree lined streets. Neighbours shop, gather and enjoy the view in the many popular cafes that line Denman and Davie Street.

False Creek

The waters under the Granville Bridge were first surveyed by Captain George Henry Richards of the Royal Navy. The land around False Creek, which remained intensely industrial until the 1950's, was later developed as an exclusive residential neighbourhood.

18

Vancouver

British Columbia's largest city and Canada's major western seaport, Vancouver welcomes over 3,000 ships from all over the world every year. Vancouver is located in southwestern British Columbia, on the Pacific Ocean, and was named after English sea captain George Vancouver, who was the first European to enter its waters in 1792. Today Vancouver is Canada's third largest city with a population of 2 million in the greater area.

Steveston

Since the 1870's, Tsawwassen has been a home to an old fishing village, named after its founder Manoah Steves. Salmon canning began in 1871 and eventually became one of the world's busiest fishing ports. Steveston, the home to Canada's largest commercial fishing fleet, is located east of Richmond on the Georgia Strait.

19

Greater Vancouver

Maple Ridge

Located one hour east of Vancouver, Maple Ridge is situated in the heart of Fraser Valley. The city is the fifth oldest municipality in British Columbia. The town's earliest settlers engaged in forestry and agriculture and today Maple Ridge is a rapidly growing industrial and agricultural center. In the aerial picture is the Fraser River, Maple Ridge and part of Fort Langley.

Fort Langley

The historic Fort Langley is a picturesque pastoral town east of Vancouver, established in 1827 by the British Hudson's Bay Company. Fort Langley is a town rich with history, offering a glimpse into the oldest European settlement in the Pacific Northwest. Today, the rough-hewn structure of Fort Langley is a National Historic Site, evoking the spirit of the frontier. Pictured here is St. George Church.

Fraser Valley

Abbotsford

British Columbia's fifth largest municipality, Abbotsford was laid out in 1889. The name comes from Harry Abbot, the general superintendent of the Canadian Pacific Railway. Today, Abbotsford has 130,000 residents and is well known for commodities such as dairy, cattle, vegetables and its famous raspberries. The city hosts a number of annual events and festivals including the Abbotsford International Airshow in August, attracting some of the world finest pilots and planes. The Berry Festival is held in July and the very popular Garlic Festival is in August. Pictured here is Sumas Mountain, the newly-developed Abbotsford neighbour Yale and a beautifully lit Mount Baker, the most visible landmark in Fraser Valley. The second picture shows the Mighty Fraser Bud Pro Rodeo, held in August as part of the Abbotsford Agrifair, the largest summer agricultural fair in British Columbia.

21

Fraser Valley

Chilliwack, Sardis

The busy and friendly community of Sardis is located on the southern side of the Trans-Canada Highway. The first picture shows Sardis and in the background Fraser Valley with nearby neighbouring villages. Nestled in the upper Fraser Valley, Chilliwack is an important industrial and agricultural part of the Lower Mainland. A major attraction is the Chilliwack Fall Exhibition, held in mid-August. A diorama of the Battle of Waterloo is displayed in the Royal Canadian Engineers Military Museum. The Landing Leisure Centre with its aquatic centre, aerobic studio and fitness centre is popular family destination. A new clock tower complements the courthouse located at Five Corners. The second picture shows the Chilliwack campus of the University College of the Fraser Valley.

22

Harrison Lake

Harrison Lake is the most sought out summer destination by locals in the Fraser Valley. The lake offers countless views and beautiful beaches. This spring picture of Harrison Lake, Long Island and Mount McRae was taken from Cogburn Beach near Beach Creek. Mineral hot springs, rich with sulphur and potash were discovered in 1859. Water cooled to 37°C is piped into three indoor and outdoor pools. Popular summer festivals near the lake include the World Championship Sand Sculpture Competition and the Festival of Arts.

Saint Thomas

The lovely architecture of Saint Thomas Episcopalian Church, located in Chilliwack near Young Road and First Avenue.

23

Cheam Peak

A bridge on the Agassiz-Rosedale Highway, the Fraser River, Ferry Island, Cheam Peak and Lady Peak are pictured in this early spring photograph. The shot was taken from the northern bank of the Fraser River near Whorlley Lane in Agassiz.

Mission, Hatzik

Mission is located near the Fraser River. In 1861 a French priest named Father Fouquet founded the St. Mary's Indian Residential School on the site, where downtown Mission is now. In the centre of Fraser Valley rests a 1,500 metre thick layer of rich soil, which the river carried into British Columbia's interior plateau over 50 million years ago, which explains the area's rich agricultural life. Matsqui Prairie, the largest agriculture area in the Fraser Valley, is covered in vegetable fields, dairy farms, hazelnuts orchards and corn fields.

24

Fishing by Hope

Sockeye season opens on the Fraser River roughly in the first week of August. Hundreds of anglers gather along the river's beaches and islands, struggling for the best spots. Millions of sockeye and king salmon spawn in the Fraser River and its tributaries, bringing good fishing for sports and commercial fishermen alike.

Hope Slide

Johnson Peak is an infamous point on Manson Ridge, just 15 kilometres from Hope. In January 1965 its snow covered stones became a grave for four people in their three cars, who stopped near the ridge during the worst possible time of the snow storm. A massive landslide of 60 million cubic yards and a 60-metre depth of stone, trees and mud swept through the valley of Nicolum Creek and across the highway. The extent of the damage is still clearly visible in this picture.

25

Fraser Valley

Fraser Canyon

British Columbia's longest river springs from Mount Robson Provincial Park under Simon Peak. The Fraser River's journey through British Columbia covers over 1350 kilometres before emptying into the Pacific Ocean near Richmond.

Bridal Falls

Chilliwack's most striking sight is the 122-metre high Bridal Veil Falls. A ten minute hike from the parking lot leads visitors to the base of the impressive cascade. At the lowest part, the waterfall is a 25-metre high curtain of water. The picnic area and hiking trails in the forest around the falls offer the more adventurous family recreation for the whole day. Bridal Falls are 17 kilometres from Chilliwack, and the entrance is from the junction of Highways #1 and #9

26

Hell's Gate

An impressive autumn view of the Fraser Canyon at the canyon's narrowest (about 30 metres wide) point. The gorge here is 180 metres deep and the river moves at 7 metres per second. Hell's Gate is a popular tourist stop and the opposite bank of the river can be reached using the Hell's Gate Airtram. A bypass around turbulent waters for spawning salmon was constructed in 1945 with the use of fish ladders.

Anderson Trestle

Two railways follow the Fraser River: the Canadian Pacific and the Canadian National. This picture of the railway bridge was taken near the Anderson River. Nearby Boston Bar was a popular midway stop between Lytton and Yale during the Fraser Gold Rush of 1858.

27

Fraser Valley

Goat Range

The rugged mountain terrain of Goat Range Provincial Park is located between Arrow and Duncan lakes. The 80,000 hectare park is a land of untamed rivers, clear lakes and fast flowing streams. This is the only place in British Columbia where white hued grizzly bears can be observed.

Kaslo

The oldest incorporated community in the Kootenays, originally staked as a sawmill site in 1889, Kaslo is set on a delta of the Kaslo River near the Purcell Mountains. In 1890 lots with rich silver deposits were sold and in five years silver ore mining boosted the population to 3,000. Several wooden municipal buildings, such as the City Hall built in 1898 and shown in this picture, were protected as National Historic Sites. Another attraction is the sternwheeler S. S. Moyie, which now graces the downtown shoreline.

28

Kokanee Creek

The West Kootenays is the home to the 235-hectare Kokanee Creek Provincial Park. The west arm of Kootenay Lake creates the Kokanee Creek. Its beautiful beaches are sought out by both tourists and Nelson residents.

Nelson

The area around Nelson is considered to be one of the best winter sport areas in North America. Nelson itself, located in the hills of West Arm Provincial Park, above the West Arm's Kootenay Lake, is a city rich with history. Gold and silver were found here in 1867 and the young town grew quickly as a result of the mining activity. Architect Francis Rattenbury, known for his exquisite design of the Parliament Buildings, designed several chateau style civic buildings here.

29

Central Kootenay

Kootenay Lake

This winter picture of Kootenay Lake was taken near the shore named Kootenay Lane.

Fort Steele

The settlement of Galbraith's Ferry was established in 1864, during the Kootenay Gold Rush. Later the place was named after Sam Steele, who peacefully settled relations between the Ktunaxa people and new white settlers. Fort Steele was a commercial centre until 1900, when the Southern railway bypassed the fort and the young town declined into obscurity. Nearby Cranbrook become the centre of the region and the Province of British Columbia reconstructed the historic town. Popular events include the Wild Horse Theatre and the historic celebration of Canada Day on July 1st. Other special events include sheep herding and horse-farming demonstrations.

30

Fernie Ridge

Located on the southern slopes of the Rocky Mountains, Fernie Ridge and Fernie Alpine Resort is a favourite winter destination for skiers and nature lovers. Over twenty large recreational facilities, chalets, hotels and a number of lodges and cottages are spread throughout the city and among the mountain slopes and ski lifts. Snow conditions are excellent on the ridge from November until early May. The town, which is named after William Fernie, an instrumental developer of the coal mining industry, has a strong history in coal mining.

Elk River

Close to Fernie, in Morrissey Ridge flows the Coal River. The canyon of the Marten River is in the larger picture, while the smaller shows the Elk River.

31

East Kootenay

Mt. Fitzwilliam

Standing majestically before the entrance to the Canadian Rockies, Mount Fitzwilliam is 2,901 metres high. The Canadian Rockies, which are shared between Alberta and British Columbia, rise in northern British Columbia near the Yukon, where they meet the Cassiar and Mackenzie Mountains before stretching along the British Columbia-Alberta border into Montana in the United States.

Mt. Terry Fox

Dedicated to the memory of the heroic Terry Fox, this beautiful peak rises to 2,650 metres. Terry Fox was a sports enthusiast and athlete who was diagnosed with cancer and lost his right leg at age 18. Three years later, he ran 5,373 kilometres across Canada on a prosthetic leg to raise money for cancer research. Terry Fox finally succumbed to cancer in 1981.

Fraser-Fort George

Canadian Rockies

The highest point of British Columbia's Rocky Mountains is Mount Robson. Several trails on and around Mount Robson offer entrancing views and high-performance sport, especially the Berg Lake Trail, which leads hikers to the peak of Mount Robson.

The largest part of the Canadian Rockies is between Alberta's Jasper and Banff. Mount Robson, 3,954 metres high, is in both pictures on this page. The ice field on its dramatic slopes is some 30 metres thick.

Mt. Robson

Mount Robson Provincial Park was established in 1913 and occupies 2,172 square kilometers of land. The name 'Canadian Rockies' is usually used for the centre and largest part of the Canadian Rockies, from Jasper to Banff, while the name 'Rocky Mountains' is used for the whole range.

33

Fraser-Fort George

Cariboo Lake

Cariboo Lake can be found in Quesnel Highlands, 25 kilometres north of Likely on Keithly Creek Road.

Cottonwood

Cottonwood House Historic Site built in 1865 is located on the Cariboo Waggon Road, on the way to North Cariboo and Barkerville. An interesting collection of wonderfully preserved houses and barns is a Government of British Columbia Historic Site. There is also a cafe, gift shop and General Store with a restaurant, offering delicious old fashioned dishes. Roadhouse, operated by the Boyd family until 1951, was an age old hotel serving miners heading from Vancouver to Barkerville, or traveling through the Gold Rush Trail to the Cariboo goldfields in the 1800s. Roadhouses were commonly distanced one day's journey from one another.

34

Williams Lake

The famous Williams Lake Stampede is not the only local attraction in this beautiful area. Thousands of tourists travel to Williams Lake to spend time in the 'Hub of the Cariboo', or travel west to Cariboo Country, Chilcotin and the Bella Coola Valley, or higher up to Prince George, Dawson Creek, the Northern Rockies, Muncho Lake and Yukon. Williams Lake offers a myriad of activities and outdoor adventures such as fishing, canoeing and hiking.

Valemount

The small but charming community of Valemount is located on the western slopes of the Canadian Rockies, on the way to Jasper and Prince George. Tourists will enjoy its natural scenery and alpine setting. Valemount belongs to the Fraser-Fort George Region.

35

Cariboo

Barkerville, Wells

This historic town, famous during the Golden Rush era, is hidden deeply in the Cariboo forest, some 80 kilometres east from Quesnel. The history began in 1858, when gold was found in a stream later named Williams Creek, by William Dietz. The growing village was then named after England's prospector Billy Barker, who found a good deposit of gold downstream. In 1865 the Cariboo Wagon Road was completed and over the next 8 years some 100,000 traveled to the city, which was sadly destroyed by fire in 1868. Thankfully, several large companies invested in the city and a few months after the tragedy some 100 buildings were rebuilt. Now, the town, known as the largest historic site in western North America, attracts thousands with 125 well-maintained buildings, restaurants, gift shops and mining demonstrations. A few kilometres west is historic Wells, shown in the smaller photo.

36

Cariboo

Prince George

Known as the gateway to the north, the logging and paper pulp city of Prince George is located almost in the exact geographical centre of British Columbia, at the confluence of the Fraser and Nechako Rivers. Today the city has a population of 80,000 and considers itself the Capital of Northern British Columbia. Although the first Europeans arrived in the area in 1793, the history of Fort George didn't begin until 1807 when Simon Fraser established it as a fur trading post and named it after King George III. Prince George began to prosper after a railroad to Prince Rupert was completed in 1914. Today, the city is the third largest in the province. Interesting places to visit include the Native Art Gallery, the Fraser-Fort George Regional Museum and the Two Rivers Gallery, pictured here. Since 1994 Prince George has been a home to the University of Northern British Columbia, shown in the second photograph.

37

Fraser-Fort George

Lac des Roches

This picture shows Lac-des-Roches, located in the hills near Highway #24, close to Bride Lake Provincial Park.

Quesnel

Quesnel, also known as "The Gold Pan City," is one of the oldest log and paper pulp cities in British Columbia. Built in the 1860's as a settlement called Quesnel Mouth at the junction of the Fraser and Quesnel Rivers, the city first centered around two hotels, a few stores, a telegraph, a grist and lumber mills. Now Quesnel has a population of 12,000 and its main industries are paper pulp, lumber and agriculture. One of several local attractions is understandable Quesnel Pulp & Plywood Mill Tours, and the 1859 log structure of Hudson Bay's store still attracts visitors to Quesnel.

Pine Valley

Pine Valley is located in the Hart Ganges, close to the Chetwynd. The area is near the foothills where the Rocky Mountains begin to rise. The Pine River flows through the valley and overhead runs the Alaska Highway.

Mackenzie

The small town of Mackenzie was built in 1966, when the dam on the Peace River was constructed. Created by the dam, Williston Lake is the largest man-made lake on the North American continent. Mackenzie is cradled between the Omenica Mountains to the west and the Rocky Mountains to the east and is located at the southern end of Williston Lake. A home to over 5,000 residents, Mackenzie's economy is primarily dependent on the forest industry and mining. One can find the world's largest tree crusher in Mackenzie.

39

Peace River

Alaska Highway

As a part of US defense, the Alaska Highway was built as a supply road after the Japanese attack on Pearl Harbour in 1941. Completed in 8 months in 1942 by 10,000 American troops and 15,000 civilians, the highway is now renowned as one of the most scenic routes in British Columbia. This picture shows the highway by Liard River. The picture on next page was taken in Dawson Creek and shows the Mile '0' marker of the highway. The highway is in excellent condition and runs 2,500 kilometres from Dawson Creek through British Columbia's Northern Rockies to Yukon's Whitehorse and then to Fairbanks, Alaska.

Kinuseo Falls

The Murray River flows through Hart Range, creating Kinuseo Falls, some 70 metres high.

40

©JH Fine Art Photo

Chetwynd

Chetwynd, a small community located in Peace River Country, stands within the picturesque foothills of the eastern slope of the Rocky Mountains. Nearby is the largest coal deposit in the world. The Chetwynd Mountains are in this picture.

Dawson Creek

In 1897 Dr. George Mercer Dawson found that the area was extremely well-suited to agriculture. The small farming community eventually turned into a regional centre when the town was connected by railways in1932 and later when it was chosen as the starting point for the 2,500 kilometre Alaska Highway. Today the main industries in Dawson Creek are oil, natural gas and agriculture.

41

Northern Rockies

A vibrant and dynamic region of crystal clear streams and lakes with all species of fish, beautiful mountains with spectacular hiking, hot springs, wildlife watching and canoeing. To reach spots like the one shown here, hikers don't need to hire helicopters or use organized tours. Thousands of beautiful, wild places can be reached by short hiking trips. This picture of the Toad River was taken between Muncho Lake and the Liard River.

Tutshi Lake

Tutshi Lake is located in northern British Columbia near the South Klondike Highway, connecting Skagway in the US with Carcross in Yukon. Just off the highway are beautiful views of the lake and the Lime Mountains, the ruins of Conrad City and the remains of mining mills on the lake shore.

42

Liard River

The Liard River springs out of the Pelly Mountains in Yukon, then flows through Yukon and British Columbia before emptying in the Northwest Territory into the Mackenzie River. This picture was taken near the Coal River community.

Hot Springs

The second largest hot springs in Canada are located in Liard River Hot Springs Provinicial Park. Nestled within a beautiful natural setting, both Alpha and 3-metre deep Beta pools offer water between 42°C and 52°C and was originally known as 'Tropical Valley'. Many travelers stop here to soak their tired bodies after long hikes, and locals from nearby communities frequent the springs as well. The nearest camping park has 53 campsites with basic facilities and is open year round.

43

Northern Rockies

© Josef Hanus

Muncho Lake

Muncho Lake Provincial Park is located in the Northern Rockies between the Toad River and the Liard River. Fine stone beaches are pleasant for both campers and anglers. Several recreational facilities and hotels provide accommodation in this beautiful area, which offers fishing, hiking and canoeing. The park has two campgrounds and several, wilder campsites off the beaten path. A good stock of lake trout and char live in the crisp, blue waters of Muncho Lake. The size of the trout is 40-60 centimetres. The water colour is affected by copper oxides, leached from the bedrock. From mile 300 at Fort Nelson, the Alaska Highway climbs the road through Stone Mountain Park. Summit Lake on page 49 sitting at 1,295 m is the highest point of the Alaska Highway. After this, the highway passes Muncho Lake framed by the mountains, which can be seen in the smaller photo.

44

Swift River

Flowing freely just near the border with Yukon, the river connects Swan Lake with Teslin Lake.

Cluculz Lake

Situated about 70 kilometres from Prince George, this fabulous lake in the centre of British Columbia in sunny fall exposure is fully treed with spruce, fir, poplar and pine. The most excellent views of the lakes are in the fall. On the picture is Cluculz Lake's eastern end, located near the Yellowhead Highway in Bulkley-Nechalko Region.

45

Northern Rockies

Creek Provincial Park

The Alaska Highway runs through some of the most beautiful scenery of the Northern Rockies. In the picture is the Alaska Highway in Creek Provincial Park near the Racing River. When I shot this picture, it was a beautiful autumn day, with hardly any traffic. Just me and my brother Jan. What I felt was complete freedom. It always gives me great pleasure to travel and take pictures in northern British Columbia and Yukon. Every time I return home to Vancouver, I dream of returning to the North.

Muskwa Range

Glaciated peaks of the Stone Mountains are the source of the milky coloured waters of the Racing River. Muskwa Range is in the background of the river, which is a favorite destination of canoeists and sport anglers.

Stone Mountains

Stone Mountain Provincial Park covers 26,000 hectares of rocky peaks, lakes, streams and forest. Climatic conditions are rough and change rapidly. Autumn begins here earlier than in southern parts of British Columbia.

Wildlife

The high rocks and bare slopes of Stone Mountain Park are sparsely inhabited by several kinds of wildlife such as the mountain goat, stone sheep and mountain caribou. More wildlife can be expected in valleys and by the lakes, where coyote and wolf can be observed along with the golden eagle, grizzly, black bear, lynx, caribou, deer, moose and many other species of smaller animals. Thin horn sheep mostly live farther west in the Cassiar Mountains.

47

St. Elias Mountains

Truly magnificent views open up to travelers driving from Pleasant Camp to Klukshu in Yukon. Highway #3 in the picture, connecting Alaska's Haines with Yukon's Haines Junctions passes through British Columbia some 74 kilometres, where numerous pictures such as this one can be shot. These mountains define the most western part of Canada.

Atlin Lake

This crystal clear lake, located in British Columbia's Coast Mountains was the location of the richest gold strike during the great rush era. Miner's camps around the lake such as Scotia Bay and Taku were abandoned after the deposits of gold became less profitable. The town of Atlin was founded in 1898, is now a favourite centre for water sports lovers.

Summit Pass

Mount St. Paul (2,127 m), Mount St. George (2,261 m) and Mount Mary Henry (2,641 m) are the highest peaks in the Northern Rockies, located around Summit Pass which itself stands at 1,295 metres and is the highest point of the Alaska Highway.

Summit Lake

Surrounded by the peaks of the Stone Mountain range, Summit Pass and Summit Lake are located near the Alaska Highway. Favorite pursuits on the lake include fishing for small and thin trout and taking in the beauty of the numerous hiking trails. Summit Peak Trail is 10 kilometres round-trip, while the moderate Flower Spring Lake Trail is 12 kilometres round-trip. Along the trails Mountain Cariboo, Stone Sheep and even Golden Eagles can be seen.

49

Cassiar

Nestled near Limestone Peak and Mount McDame, the abandoned mining town of Cassiar is still an important part of British Columbia's history. In the past, a great deal of Chrysolite Asbestos came from Cassiar. The mine, which once employed 450 workers, closed in 1992 after 42 years of operation and the close-knit community of Cassiar was forced to pack up and leave, some staying in British Columbia, while others scattered to other parts of the world. The majority of homes were bull-dozed or trucked away, but some remain occupied, however there is no electricity or any modern services.

Mt. McDame

This picture shows the remains of Cassiar under Mount McDame, where rich deposits of Chrysolite Asbestos were found.

50

Mt. Pendleton

Rising above Good Hope Lake, 2,164 metre high Mount Pendleton is located in the Cassiar Mountain Range and hosted a gold rush in the 1870s.

Cassiar Highway

The 725 kilometre Stewart-Cassiar Highway joins with the Yellowhead Highway at the Skeena River Bridge. Originally a logging and mining haul road, the highway is now half paved and half gravel. Since the road has been improved, the road is fine for small cars, motor homes and towing trailers. Travelers will experience the beauty of mountain scenery and wild lakes as they travel along this stretch, and may even be lucky enough to spot some grizzlies feeding on salmon. Be sure not to miss the town of Stewart and its neighbour Hyder in Alaska.

Stikine

Dease Lake

The history of Dease Lake began in 1838 when a Hudson's Bay Company post was established by Robert Campbell. The community Laketon, located on the west side of the lake was a boat building centre in the time of the Cassiar Gold Rush between 1872 and 1880. Today, the area is a recreational site with great lake trout fishing. Dease Lake is also located near the Cassiar Highway. The picturesque early fall scenery near Dease Lake and Tatsho Mountains are the subject of this picture.

Jade City

The Indian village of Jade City, population 12, is one of a few communities located near the Cassiar Highway. The city was named for the jade deposits found in the area, which tourists can buy at the town's Jade Store. The area is still rich with minerals such as gold, jade and asbestos.

52

Simons Lake

Simons Lake located near the Cassiar Highway offers challenging hiking into the nearby mountains.

Telegraph Creek, Stikine

The Stikine River, famous for its trophy sized king salmon flows through a spectacular remote area. Telegraph Creek Road is a challenging venture up to the Stikine Canyon. This provincial recreational area is a draw for hardy tourists who come to enjoy its wild nature. Traditionally, the Stikine region was the home to the Tahltan tribe. The history trades back to Klondike Gold Rush of the late 19th century. The discovery of gold in the Stikine River during the 1860s brought more settlers and the construction of telegraph lines gave the community its name. This autumn picture was taken near 40 Mile Flats.

53

Kitimat-Stikine

Tatshenshini–Alsek

Kluane National Park and its extremely wild Tatshenshini-Alsek Park are spread across British Columbia and Alaska. This vast, unbroken ecological land covers 97,000 square kilometres. Without roads or trails, the park is a land where vast and wild rivers cut their way through the rough nature, creating valley and canyons. There is an extensive wildlife population and excellent fishing, however the rivers, some of North America's wildest, are not easily accessible.

Skeena Mountains

The pristine wilderness of the Skeena Mountains, a paradise for nature lovers, hunters, hikers and anglers is imposing and heavily glaciated. Many lakes and rivers with excellent stocks of fish are only accessible by plane or helicopter.

54

Cambria Icefield

Mezidan Lake Provincial Park is the home to Cambria Icefield and the town of Stewart. The Bear River Glacier, a part of the Cambria Icefield was photographed in Bear Pass. Stewart is located on the Alaska-British Columbia border, on a spur of the Cassiar Highway and the head of Portland Canal. The town is nestled in a deep harbour and is Canada's northernmost ice-free port. Located near Stewart, the community of Hyder in Alaska is renowned for its local grain alcohol, the potent Everclear. Locals enjoy watching visitors 'get Hyderized' upon drinking a single shot of the liquor. Hyder is also popular for grizzly bear watching.

Bear Glacier

The Bear River and the mountains of Bear Glacier Provincial Park are in the smaller picture.

55

Stikine

Burns Lake

The northern gateway to the untamed wilderness of Tweedsmuir Park, Burns Lake is located near the Yellowhead Highway. The local history reaches back to 1866, when a trapper named Barney Mulvaney settled here. Massive settlement began in 1911 when the railway construction crews begin work. 40 years later some 90 sawmills were operating in the area.

Fort Fraser

A fur trading post was established here by explorer Simon Fraser in 1806. The history of the settlement of Fort Fraser is connected with the Grand Truck Pacific Railway. In April 1914, the last spike of this railway was driven here. Fraser Lake offers good accommodation and great fishing in the summer months. One of the oldest settlements is located west of Prince George near Highway #16.

56

Bulkley-Nechalko

Moricetown Canyon

The Bulkley River flows through Moricetown Canyon, where natives catch salmon with nets and gaff poles to feed their families. The place is close to the historic village of Moricetown, which was built by natives several thousand years ago.

Smithers

Bulkley Valley is home to Smithers, a town of 5,500 people which was incorporated in 1921. The picture shown here was taken near Smithers of the close hills of Hudson Bay Mountain, where one can find ideal terrain for cross country skiing, while its higher peaks contain beautiful downhill ski slopes. Other recreational opportunities are fishing, hiking and in the winter months snowmobiling. The town's name comes from Sir Alfred Smithers, the chairman of the Grand Truck Pacific Railway.

57

Bulkley-Nechalko

Prince Rupert

The north coast city of Prince Rupert is known as the place where bears, moose, eagles and whales outnumber local residents. As the northernmost BC Ferries port, Prince Rupert is located on the Tsimpsean Peninsula, where the Skeena River empties into Chatham Sound. This ice-free harbour is the connection to the Queen Charlotte Island and to Vancouver Island. The port is called the 'Halibut Capital of the World,' due to the annual catch of over 7,000 tons.

Queen Charlotte Island

Queen Charlotte Island is located north of Vancouver Island. The area can be reached by BC Ferries from Prince Rupert. The falls under Mosquito Lake on Moresby Island is the subject of this picture.

58

Babine Mountains

The Yellowhead Highway stretches 700 kilometres from Prince George to Prince Rupert. It is a beautiful trip through a gently rolling plateau with numerous lakes, untamed wilderness and fascinating towns and villages. The Bulkley and Morice Rivers are famous names among anglers for excellent salmon and steelhead fishing.

Francois Lake

Sockeye salmon spawn some 1,000 kilometres from the Pacific Ocean to the Skeena and Bulkley Rivers, before finally reaching Francois Lake after 30 days. Francois Lake is located south of Burns Lake, surrounded by the hills of the Uncha Mountains in Red Hills Provincial Park. Along with beautiful fishing and wildlife watching, it is possible to engage in many sports activities.

59

Bulkley-Nechalko

Tweedsmuir Park

The Coast Mountains are home to Tweedsmuir Provincial Park, which is split into northern and southern halves. In the north is parkland bound by Ootsa and Whitestail Lakes while the southern part touches the Coast Mountains near the 3,533 metre high Mount Monarch. The Freedom Highway passes the park from Williams Lake to Bella Coola. As British Columbia's largest park Tweedsmuir Park covers 995,000 hectares and is the most diverse of Canada's parks with rivers, deep canyons, clear lakes, mountains and glaciers which attract hikers, canoeists and mountain bikers. Lonesome Lake is a winter home to 500 trumpeter swans.

Burke Channel

North Bentinck Arm and the Burke Channel connect Bella Coola's port with the Pacific Ocean.

60

Cariboo

Mt. Saugstad

The picture of Mount Saugstad (2,908 m), standing above Bella Coola in the Coast Mountains, was taken from the highest point of Heckman Pass.

Heckman Pass

The gate to the Bella Coola Valley, Heckman Pass is a dramatic and unforgiving part of the partially gravel 'Freedom Highway.' Bella Coola's infamous 'Hill' is the point on Highway #20 where the Chilkotin Plateau ends. At its highest elevation of 1,524 metres, the highway passes through Tweedsmuir Park at a steep angle, splitting the park into its southern and northern regions. Heckman Pass and the highway are open all year round. Heckman Pass, constructed in 1953 as the last part of Highway #20, opened up Bella Coola Valley's residents to greater freedom and also allowed connection with Williams Lake.

61

Central Coast

Bella Coola

The Atnarko River and snowcapped Mount Marvin were shot under Heckman Pass in Tweedsmuir Provincial Park. The history of Bella Coola Valley at the metting of Bella Coola River and the Pacific, involves a group of Norwegian Lutherans from Minnesota who were given land grants to live there and, after discovering the land well suited to agriculture, established the village of Hagensborg in the 1890s. This fishing and lumber community here was founded in 1894 by Americans who had escaped America during the depression. One hundred years before, Captain George Vancouver moored his vessel in the Burke Channel and in the same year, fur trader Alexander Mackenzie passed through the same area completing the first recorded crossing of the continent. The Bella Coola Valley is now the home to 1800 people. The second picture shows the Acwsalcta First Nation School in Bella Coola.

62

Eagle Lake

The Cariboo region is a favourite part of British Columbia, visited by thousands of tourists every summer. Imposing snowcapped mountains rise above lakes where clear water attracts hikers and canoeists. Some trailheads are accessible only by canoe. The lake has open meadow BCFS campsites from which cartop boats can be launched. Eagle Lake is located near Highway #20, some three hours west of Williams Lake.

Klinaklini River

The Kilinaklini River flows along the Pacific Ranges and empties its clear waters into the Queen Charlotte Strait. The Cariboo region has many rivers offering good trout and Dolly Pardon fishing. This picture was taken near Kleena Kleene.

63

Cariboo

Anahim Lake

Autumn yields stunning colours in the Cariboo, where Anahim Lake is nestled. Numerous lakes and streams offer good fishing and excellent hunting. The area is a regular summer destination for British Columbia's residents and tourists, who spend weekends and summer vacations in the numerous cottages scattered around the countless pristine lakes. One of these pristine jewels, Williams Lake, holds its infamous Williams Lake Stampede, which allows access to the tree mountain ranges in this area, is held every July.

Tatla Lake

The small community of Tatla Lake, located three hours west of Williams Lake, is known as the trailhead to Tatlayoko Lake, the Homathko Icefield and the highest peak in British Columbia, the 4,016 metre high Mount Waddington.

64

Cariboo

Lac la Hache

This countryside scene was taken close to Lac la Hache, some 30 kilometres south of 150 Mile House.

Riske Creek

Romantically positioned old ranches can be seen in the hills and plateau of 'Cowboy Country,' as the Cariboo Chilkotin region is often called. Some are still active, however most have been abandoned, as well as several trapper's cabins in the area. Some old communities such as Redstone, Hansville, Alexis Creek and Riske Creek are located near Bull Canyon and the Chilko River in the Bald Mountains. An interesting note is that over 500 California Big Horn Sheep live on a 450 hectare Provincial Game Preserve, located within the Interior Plateau, east of South Tweedsmuir Provincial Park. Riske Creek, where this picture was taken, is the site of the earliest established ranches.

65

Cariboo

Cowboy Country

Bull Canyon and the Chilko River are pictured near Alexis Creek. There is a romantic camping site, nestled some 110 kilometres from Williams Lake.

Cariboo Chilcotin

The Chilcotin region, located west of Williams Lake and nicknamed 'Cowboy Country,' spreads across a 5,000 square kilometre plateau between the Fraser River (in the picture) and the Coast Mountains. Since 1860 when white settlement began, cattle ranching has been the main industry for all communities in the area. Cattle roam freely in Chilkotin areas and one has to keep an eye out for them on the roads. Cowboy skills are often performed in villages and there is fierce competition every July at the Williams Lake Stampede where antiquated techniques such as steer wrestling, cattle roping and bull riding are showcased.

66

Peace Canyon

Peace Canyon, in Peace Reach, famous for the W.A.C. Bennett Dam, one of the world's largest earth-filled structures, which was completed in 1967. During the construction skeleton parts of plesiosaur, which swam here 100 million years ago, as well as prehistoric bird footprints, were found.

Coquihalla Summit

The Coquihalla Highway #5 is a well monitored and maintained toll highway. Near Merritt you can turn right into Highway #97C which runs to Okanagan. In Hope, where the toll highway begins, drivers can select other, more scenic versions to reach Manning Park, Okanagan and Kelowna, using Highway #3. Coquihalla Highway Summit is located in the Thompson-Nicola Region.

67

Peace River

Kamloops

The unofficial capital of inland British Columbia, Kamloops is located at the confluence of the two Thompson Rivers. The history dates back to 1811 when the first Europeans arrived. Hudson's Bay Company built a post in 1821 to control fur trade. The Gold Rush of the 1860's and the Canadian Pacific Railway brought in more residents, however by 1893 the population was still only 500. Now, the city is an important industrial and mining centre with a population of 86,000 residents. Hiking, fishing and skiing are major outdoor activities, countering a rich cultural life, including the Kamloops Symphony Orchestra, the Art Gallery and Western Canada Theatre Company.

Kamloops Lake

Kamloops Lake, a popular recreation reservoir on the Thompson River is nestled in the valley just a few kilometres west of Kamloops.

68

Thompson-Nicola

Columbia Mountains

Driving from Kamloops to the Canadian Rockies, the most interesting landmark is the North Thompson River, however, the lovely Columbia Mountains, photographed on this page near Adams Lake, will charm you as well. The Thompson River continues to run along the highway as you head to Blue River and Valemount.

Three Valley

A collection of historic buildings, including a saloon, school house, church, trapper's cabin and more is located in Three Valley. This tranquil retreat named 'Three Valley Gap' was founded in 1960 by the Gordon Bell family. A modern resort including a 200 room chateau-motel, restaurants and a museum, Three Valley is located in a beautiful park between the sheer cliffs of Monashee Mountains and the clear waters of Three Valley Lake.

69

Columbia-Shuswap

Swan Lake

Surrounded by ranches and orchards, Swan Lake is located close to Vernon, under Silver Star Mountain. Vernon is nestled in the North Okanagan between Kalamalka and Swan Lakes. The town's history is dating to 1811, when first fur traders arrived. Then in 1850 gold was discovered at Mission Creek and along the east part of Okanagan Lake. Father Durieu built a cabin by Swan Lake and Cornelius O'Keffe established his ranch in 1867. Forestry and agriculture are major industries in this area and numerous ranches are spread around Vernon, as well as Swan and Okanagan Lakes.

Skaha Lake

Beautiful beaches encircle the lakes of Okanagan. This picture was taken from Skaha Lake near Penticton in the Okanagan-Similkameen Region.

70

Kelowna

The heart of the Okanagan Valley, Kelowna is a major rapidly growing city in British Columbia. Its economy is driven by fruit farming, wine and juice production and tourism. The region produces 30% of all apples harvested in Canada.

Myra Canyon

The world famous Myra Canyon is near Kelowna, where the former Kettle Valley Railway operated until 1973. The railway was constructed on the canyon's extremely sheer hillsides in the 1910s by Andrew McCulloch. Within the space of 9 kilometres 18 trestles were built from local wood. In August 2003 a huge fire destroyed 12 of the trestles. The reconstruction of one of British Columbia's most beautiful attractions started almost immediately and today almost all of the trestles are rebuilt.

71

Silver Star

World class winter conditions are offered by all of British Columbia's mountains. Okanagan offers gentle slopes and rolling hills, and ideal terrain for snowboarding. Silver Star, located near Vernon, offers both good terrain for cross-country skiing and moderate runs for advanced skiers. Wide open friendly slopes and a colourful Victorian-themed village make Silver Star North America's best small resort.

Big White

Okanagan winter sport activity can be provided in the Big White Mountains, located some 50 kilometres east of Kelowna. The area is second only to the ski giant of Whistler. Big White, with its 24 foot snowfall and over 100 runs, ranging from beginner to expert, is the finest ski destination in the Kootenay Boundary Region.

72

North Okanagan

Okanagan Valley

Apple orchards and vineyards surround the valley where Kaladent, Pentincton, Summerland, Peachland and Kelowna are nestled by Okanagan Lake and Skaha Lake. The first settlers in 1859 came with Charles Pandosy and started to plant fruit trees and vineyards, sowing the seeds of the lucrative industries of fruit farming and wine production of today. This picture shows a golf course and vineyard near Kelowna.

Summerland

The South Okanagan region, including the town of Summerland, can be seen from Giant's Head Mountain. This lovely town, surrounded by apple, peach and apricot orchards has several historic buildings and churches. The town's history is connected with the Kettle Valley Railroad, the construction of which began in 1910.

73

Enderby

The Shuswap River, flowing in the North Okanagan region near the town of Endernear is illustrated in this beautiful fall scene. An interesting landmark of this site is the Endernear Cliffs. Some 50 millions years ago volcanic lava covered the greater part of the area from south of Kamloops to Endernear. The cliffs loom just above the river.

Douglas Lake

Dry yellow low hills in the centre of the region are home to several beautiful lakes, including the trout-stocked Douglas Lake shown in this picture. In late afternoon, the sun creates a plastic effect on the hills and the lake transforms to a dark blue. The village nearby is dusted with a few homes and a small church. Nearby is the town of Nicola, which was settled in the 1800s in Nicola Valley. Douglas Lake belongs to Thompson-Nicola Region.

North Okanagan

Bromley Rock

The Similkameen River stretches to the mountains close to Bromley Rock. Gold was discovered in 1897 and the nearby town of Hendley became one of the greatest names in Canadian mining history. Fifty thousand ounces of gold per year spewed from Nickel Plate mine, increasing to 1.5 million ounces of gold and 4 million pounds of copper after the Mascot Fraction joined in the production. In 1955 the ore ran out and today only the golden river banks remain in memory of a distant golden age.

Penticton

The city of Penticon is nestled on dramatic clay cliffs and bordered near Okanagan and Skaha Lakes. Penticonians take full advantage of the dual lakes.

75

Keremeos

Nestled in the warm Similkameen Valley, Keremeos is a fruit growing town and one can often see many decorated fruit stands posted near the highway. Mild winters, friendly countryside, year round sunshine and low precipitation makes this place interesting for retirees. In the picture is the historic Grist Mill, built in 1877 by Barrington Price. It is the last pioneer flour mill with the original construction and machinery, and today stands as a living and working museum. Other main industries in Keremeos are cattle ranching, gardening and wine production.

Dominion Observatory

Huge radio telescopes are located in Twin Lake Valley, where the Dominion Radio Astrophysical Observatory is based. The structure is ringed by mountains, which protect the telescopes from interfering radio signals.

76

Osoyoos

The southeast part of the Okanagan Valley is the home of Osoyoos Lake. The Okanagan Valley, created by glaciers thousands of years ago, is the northern tip of the Sonoran Desert, which begins in the far south of Mexico. The Osoyoos Desert is Canada's only hot desert region. The Baldy Mountains around the valley create a beautiful frame for Haynes Point Provincial Park located on Osoyoos Lake. There Osoyoos Lake splits in two near the narrow sand spit, which is home to a very popular camping site.

Bridesville

An encompassing view of Anarchist Mountain can be achieved from the highest point of the Crowsnest Highway, above the Osoyoos Valley. On this page is an autumn scene of a small community of farms and cottages. The mountainside slopes are also the home to Bridesville in the Kootenay Boundary Region.

Okanagan-Similkameen

Manning Park

Located in the heart of the Cascade Mountains in Gibson Pass, Manning Provincial Park offers a wide range of outdoor activities. Excellent cross-country and downhill terrain renowned for its dry snow, 25 marked trails and four ski lifts, make the region attractive for all winter-sport activities. The Lightning Lakes are magnetic in the summer months to families and Similkameen River is popular for anglers. Scenic mountains such as Three Brothers or Thunder Lake are fine destinations for hikers.

Greenwood

Greenwood is known as the smallest town in British Columbia, located near Highway #3. Walking around old houses and restaurants, one can still feel the atmosphere of a bygone age. The town belongs to the Kootenay Boundary Region.

78

Texas Creek

Fall creates beautiful, picturesque scenery in Lillooet Valley, where the Fraser River flows to Lytton, creating excellent water conditions for white-water rafting. The pictured area, just off Cariboo Highway #12, connects with Stein Valley Provincial Park and the Stein Mountains.

Lytton

Located where the clear green waters of the Thompson River meet with the brown, silt-laden Fraser River, Lytton is famed as the 'Rafting Capital of Canada'. Other outdoor activities such as hiking, camping and fishing can be enjoyed in close proximity to the town. Fur trader Simon Fraser visited this place, known in that time as 'The Forks' in 1808. The community was renamed in 1858 in honor of British Colonial Secretary and novelist Edward Bulwer-Lytton.

79

Joffre Lake

If driving along Duffey Lake Road, leaving Pemberton and heading to Lillooet, heats your engine up, take a break and walk around the fantastically coloured Lower Joffre Lake. You will see the glacier-laden peaks of the Joffre Glacier Group steeply rising above. A hiking trail of 11 kilometres both ways will lead hikers to Middle Joffre Lake and Upper Joffre Lake. By the time you return to the parking lot, your engine will be cold again and ready to go.

Cayoosh Range

Hundreds of beautiful scenic points will stop you en route to Lillooet from Pemberton. You'll witness rivers, mountains and lakes and even have the option of staying overnight on some of the quiet and wild campsites. The last part of Duffey Lake Road before Lilooet is really picturesque, showcasing Mount Brew, colourful Cayoos Creek and Seton Lake.

80

Marble Canyon

Heading from Lillooet to the north, the Fraser River and the surrounding mountains create charming sights in Edge Hill Provincial Park. This picture was taken near 'Fountain' on the southern edge of the Marble Canyon. Driving some 20 kilometres north, one cannot avoid the beautiful scenery of the canyon and Pavilion Lake with campsites. This area belongs to Marble Canyon Provincial Park.

Spences Bridge

The Thompson River is the wild stretch of water which follows you from Lytton to Spences Bridge and Catche Creek. This picture was taken in August, when millions of sockeye salmon spawn from the Pacific Ocean to the Fraser River and then into the Thompson River. In the picture is a place where salmon used to be caught with gaff poles and nets by natives.

81

Thompson-Nicola

Joffre Peak

Joffre Peak is located some 20 kilometres south of Pemberton and can be seen from the spot where Duffey Lake Road passes through Cayoosh Pass. On the left of snowy Joffre Peak is Chief Pascall. Joffre Peak can also be seen in the background rising above Duffey Lake.

Duffey Lake Road

Alpine views can be seen just by driving along Duffey Lake Road from Pemberton to Lillooet. Some of the mountains are over 2,900 metres. Joffre Peak is 2,721 metres; Mount Rohr, 2,423 metres; Cayoosh Mountain, 2,561 metres; Skihist Mountain, 2,968 metres and Mount Brew located close to Lilooet reaches 2,891 metres. Duffey Lake Provincial Park spreads across 2,379 hectares and was established in 1993. Duffey Road's various and curling highway is popular for motorbikers.

Squamish-Lillooet

Narin Falls

A short distance from Pemberton, Narin Falls with the Green River is a truly wild experience. The easy hiking trail near the Green River is an easy family walk which will position you in the center of a great wilderness.

Pemberton Valley

Over millions of years, the river brought rich soil to the valley, resulting in a green pocket of agricultural land, widely known for its seed potatoes. Cattle farming and other agricultural activity were provided under the snow capped Coast Mountains. In 1967 Pemberton was the first commercial producer of seed potatoes in the world. The potatoes grow with careful monitoring to ensure that they are virus free. While in town, tourists can visit the Pemberton Heritage Museum, historic hotels, and motels and spend their time golfing, camping and fishing.

83

Mt. Currie

The massive, multi-summit mountain, Mount Currie (2,591 metres), is located north of Garibaldi Park, just above Pemberton. Salish First Nations people were the first settlers at the foot of majestic Mount Currie near D'Arcy. The mountain was named for Scotsman John Currie, the first permanent non-native settler in the area. His ranch was just at the mountain's foot.

Garibaldi Provincial Park

Mountains and glaciers, rivers, impressive forests and lakes, excellent conditions for skiers and hikers: this is Garibaldi Provincial Park, in the southernmost part of the Coast Mountain Range. The park, dominated by the 2,675 metre Mount Garibaldi, is made up of 195,000 hectares of wilderness and is forested by hemlock, fir, balsam and red cedar. Wildlife that can be seen includes the black bear, mountain goat, grizzly bear, deer and wolf.

Squamish-Lillooet

Coast Mountains

The western range of the North American mainland Cordillera is the Coast Mountains and covers most of British Columbia's coast. The range starts in Yukon and ends near the Fraser Valley. The range is 1,620 kilometres long and some 190 kilometres wide. Mount Waddington, standing at 4,019 metres is the highest peak of the range (not pictured here), is located in the Pacific Ranges, close to Tatla Lake. This picture is of Spearhead Range, in northern Garibaldi Provincial Park.

Mt. Whistler

The multi-summit peak of the 2,181 metre high Mount Whistler is the most popular skiing destination in North America. The peak, located above Whistler Village near the Fitzsimmons Range, can be reached by Whistler Village Gondola or Fitzsimmons Express.

85

Squamish-Lillooet

Armchair Glacier

The Armchair Glacier, located north of the Wedge Mountain under the peaks of Mount Weart is a favourite destination for helicopter tours and skiers. The massif can be perfectly seen from the shores of Green Lake. Mount Weart is the second highest mountain with three summits.

Whistler, Green Lake

Whistler, the popular West Coast municipality of 10,000 residents, is internationally known as the finest North American winter resort. Its hotels and recreational resorts are, during winter months, overloaded with skiers, and in summer months becomes host to golfers and music festivals. Ski runs are used in the summer by bikers and hikers. This picture shows the northern part of Whistler and Green Lake, located just north of Whistler.

86

Squamish-Lillooet

ILLANAAQ

Illanaaq the Inukshuk, which has been chosen as the logo of the 2010 Vancouver Winter Olympics, stands here in stone on the peak of Whistler, facing Black Tusk. Illanaaq is the Inuktitut word for 'friend.' An Inukshuk is a traditional stone maker which the Inuit used to guide their way across the treacherous Arctic.

Fitzsimmons Range

Composed of softly rounded summits in the west and glaciated summits in the east is Fitzsimmons Range, where Whistler Mountain and ski area are located. The picture shows the eastern part of Fitzsimmons range, photographed from Little Whistler Peak. The highest peak in the centre is Overload Mountain, to its left is Mount Fitzsimmons and to the right, Flute Summit.

87

Squamish-Lillooet

Black Tusk

High above Garibaldi Lake, the most frequently photographed peak in British Columbia is Black Tusk, 2,319 metres high. The massif is an inactive volcano which formed 35 million years ago when the Juan de Fuca Plate and the Explorer Plate collided. The peak, a yearly destination of thousands of hikers, can easily be reached by several trails from Squamish and from the Whistler area. Driving from Vancouver to Whistler, you will see this peak several times briefly, but the best observation is from Whistler Peak.

Mamquam Mountains

Located south of Diamond Peak, mountains with their spawning ice-field can be seen from Squamish. The Mamquam's highest peak is 2,588 metres high. This picture was taken from the hiking trail near Mamquam Lake.

88

Tantalus Range

The heavily glaciated Tantalus Range's 306 square kilometres are located between the Ashlu River and the Squamish River. The highest peak of the range is Mount Tantalus at 2,603 metres.

Whistler

The Upper Village of Whistler is where Fairmont Chateau Whistler is nestled. Wizard Express and Magic Chair will lift skiers in minutes to the 7th Heaven Zone of Blackcomb Peak, which at 2,436 metres is higher than Mount Whistler, however the peak is not accessible, while Whistler's is. This picture is of the Main Village, where Excalibur Gondola Blackcomb, Fitzsimmons Express and Whistler Village Gondola operate.

89

Squamish

The Outdoor Recreation Capital of Canada, as Squamish calls itself, is nestled in truly spectacular scenery. The Coast Mountains and Garibaldi Park on the one side, and the ocean view from Howe Sound on the other, the excellent four-line connector of Highway #99 to Vancouver and Whistler make Squamish one of the most popular living areas in British Columbia.

Brandywine Falls

Scenic attractions can be found on Brandywine Creek, close to Daisy Lake. A short walk from the parking lot near the Sea to Sky Highway will lead you to the viewpoint above, from where the 66 metre high Brandywine Falls, just 11 kilometres south of Whistler can be observed. Daisy Lake on the left side is also clearly visible.

90

Wedge Mountains

The highest summit in Garibaldi Provincial Park, Wedge Mountain is 2,892 metres high. This picture was taken from the peak of Mount Whistler. From Green Lake Park is a 6 kilometre trail to Wedge Lake.

Chekamus River

British Columbia is truly a paradise for photographers. A picture of the Chekamus River and the co-author of this book J. M. Hanus, was taken from the trail to Black Tusk. Wild spring emerald waters are attractive for whitewater rafting and kayaking. The river, beginning in Garibaldi Park, drains the mountain snow and joins the Squamish River at Cheekeye. The streams in Squamish and Whistler offer excellent fishing, but some rivers abide by catch-and-release laws. Anglers should check local restrictions before going fishing.

91

Furry Creek

The shores of Howe Sound host Furry Creek, well known for its excellent position and golf course. Near the ocean is a small beach community called Oliver's Landing. The upper part with an excellent ocean view is located in the hills above the highway.

Squamish Harbour

The Squamish River empties into Howe Sound, creating Squamish Spit, a favourite water for kite boarders and windsurfers. It is considered one of the world's best windsurfing spots. Numerous other sports activities can be observed in Squamish. Popular events are the Test of Metal Mountain Bike Festival in June, the Squamish Triathlon, the Sea to Sky Trail Ride in July and Squamish Days Logger Sports in September.

92

Squamish-Lillooet

Mt. Fee

In the picture is the 2,162 metre high peak of Mount Fee, as can be seen from the Squamish River Valley. Famous characteristics are the two sharp blades of volcanic rock jutting from the top of the peak. Mount Fee is a member of the Pacific Ring of Fire.

Squamish River

A true outdoor adventure playground is Squamish and Paradise Valley in the Sea to Sky area, where the Squamish River and the Chekamus River flow. Rustic campsites in a wild setting or just wild sites near the rivers and creeks are favourite destinations to Vancouverites. In the summer and fall, hundreds anglers can be seen trying their luck with the spawning salmon. Over 100 kilometres long, an active gravel logging road runs along the Squamish River to Clendinnig Park, the left branch of the road continuing along to Ashlu Mountain.

93

©Josef Hanus

Shannon Falls

Rising 330 metres above Highway #99, Shannon Falls are the third highest falls in the province. The water source is the 1,700 metre granite horn Mount Habrich.

Stawamus Chief

The Chief stands guard over Howe Sound. Seven hundred metres high and 93 million years old, the massif is the second largest granite monolith in the world and is extremely popular amongst hikers and climbers. Stawamus Chief Provincial Park was established in 1997.

Howe Sound ——>next page picture

North America's southernmost fjord and a playground for Vancouverites, Howe Sound extends the Pacific Ocean to the Squamish Valley.

Squamish-Lillooet

Mt. Garibaldi

The large extinct volcano of Mount Garibaldi is the most visible landmark in this area. Located near Squamish in Garibaldi Park, its southern sharp peak is named Diamond Head. The massif is the first truly Alpine peak in the Coast Mountains to be climbed. Diamond Head was first seen in 1860 by Captain Richards, who entered Howe Sound (in the smaller picture) and named the peak after an Italian patriot Giuseppe Garibaldi.

Sea to Sky

The connector between Vancouver, Whistler and Pemberton got the nickname of 'SEA to SKY' Highway. Our next book, WHISTLER-GARIBALDI-SEA to SKY, will bring more pictures and information from this heavily visited area of British Columbia.

Squamish-Lillooet

Across Labrador, Newfoundland

By Checamus River, British Columbia

Across Liard River, NWT and in Rocky Mountains, below

Travelling Canada…

My first cross-country trip across Canada in 1999 changed my business orientation. It was some 30,000 kilometres, which I traveled with my brother John. The trip took us three months and left us a little tired, not being experienced at driving great distances while taking pictures over such a long time. During the return trip to Vancouver, just before entering British Columbia, I thought I would never undertake such a trip again, but within the last few kilometres, when I realized our trip was over, I had a change of heart. Even before I turned off the engine in front of my home, I had begun planning another Canadian trip, and I was determined to travel cross-country the following year. I asked my family, who would go with me, their thoughts. They laughed and said that I was crazy, that it was too early to think about another trip. The following spring my new Canada book became very popular, and in May I went to the Yukon, NWT and Alaska with my son Josef. On the third cross-country Canadian trip in 2001 I traveled with my son, who had become my business partner. Over the next several years we made many more trips, varying from localized trips across BC for our new British Columbia book, to longer trips focusing on the Rockies, Prairies, and as far away as Southern Ontario and Toronto.

Travelling throughout Canada has affected my sense of scale. A short trip now means about 3,000 kilometres round-trip, for example from Vancouver to the Rockies. Medium distanced trips are now to the Prairies or Toronto, a long trip goes further east to Atlantic Canada, and an extra long trip means Newfoundland and Labrador, some thirty thousand kilometres round-trip. These distances are not, of course, the most direct routes across Canada, for while taking pictures we constantly travel back and forth, to the north and south, east and west, over and over again.

After numerous medium distanced trips across British Columbia and the success of my first two books, Greater Vancouver and British Columbia, I radically reduced my ideas regarding world travel and decided to spend almost all my time in Canada. I bought a strong diesel truck, which proved to be an excellent decision for those long trips. My truck and camper are safe and comfortable for driving long distances. Each new trip has brought me ideas for new books. After the first trip across the country, I flew to the Yukon to take more autumn pictures for the Canada book. I was awed by the beauty of this northernmost part of Canada and brought back so many beautiful pictures from the Yukon that I decided to publish another book about Alaska and Yukon. Shortly after this we published books on Ontario and Atlantic Canada for similar reasons. When we prepared the British Columbia book for printing, we realized that it wasn't possible to show the beauty of this province in one single book, so we decided to publish four local titles covering British Columbia and two more titles from Ontario, Southern Ontario and Toronto.

Photographer and Publisher

The author of this book, photographer and owner of JH Fine Art Photo Ltd., Josef Hanus, is one of the most accredited and celebrated scenic and wilderness photographers in Canada and North America. He has created, using only his own photographs, and published over 150 titles of Canadian calendars since 1989. Now he is working on a long line of travel-photographic books with the theme he loves the most: Canada. As of 2008 he will have self-published 16 books, all of which have become best-sellers in their category. His award-winning photographs and best-selling Canadian calendars and photographic books have grown purely out of hard work. After graduating from a European art and photography institute, he began his career working for magazines and newspapers, and has had tens of thousands of photographs and articles published throughout Europe and North America. He continues to observe nature through the lens of his camera. Studying objects he trained his taste for scenic views and his eye to the height of artistic professionalism. But his sensitive sight.is not the only source of success. Over the years, he perfectly selected his professional partners and patiently tested cameras and lenses for his high quality work. The result of these efforts can be seen in his products. People love Josef's photographic books and calendars, because Josef loves to create them. Since 1997 he has been working with his son, Josef M. Hanus.

About the Heart: JH Fine Art Photo's published products are visibly marked with Josef's trademark, a red heart combined with Canada's maple leaf. The company logo was beautifully re-designed in 3D by Jan Hanus, who joined the company in 2007.